CW00342098

40 songs and ca
for Christmas

The Faber
Carol Book

Selected and arranged by Gwyn Arch and Ben Parry

SA(B) and piano

FABER *ff* MUSIC

© 2001 by Faber Music Ltd
First published in 2001 by Faber Music Ltd
3 Queen Square London WC1N 3AU
Corrected impression 2002
Music processed by Don Sheppard
Cover by Shireen Nathoo Design
Printed in England by Caligraving Ltd
All rights reserved

ISBN 0-571-52007-3

Permission to perform the works in this anthology in public must be obtained from
the Society duly controlling performing rights unless there is a current licence for
public performance from the Society in force in relation to the premises at which the
performance is to take place. Such permission must be obtained in the UK from
Performing Right Society Ltd, 29–33 Berners Street, London W1P 4AA, or its affiliated
Societies in each country throughout the world.

ACKNOWLEDGEMENTS

We would like to thank Sue Alexander, Mike Brewer, Stephen Clark, Hedvig Eriksson,
Howard Goodall, Peter Gritton, Roger Kendal, Ceri Lewis, Lin Marsh, John Parry,
Patrick Rooke, Don Sheppard, Errollyn Wallen, Val Whitlock and Richard Williams for
their contributions to this collection, and finally Kathryn Oswald and the team at
Faber Music.

G. A. and B. P.

To buy Faber Music publications or to find out about the full range of titles available
please contact your local music retailer or Faber Music sales enquiries:

Faber Music Limited, Burnt Mill, Elizabeth Way, Harlow, CM20 2HX England
Tel: +44 (0)1279 828982   Fax: +44(0)1279 828983
sales@fabermusic.com   fabermusic.com

PREFACE

Christmas is a time of great joy and celebration. In selecting and arranging this collection, our main aim was to capture an extensive range of moods at Christmas time – from the celebratory to the awe-inspired, the humorous to the more reflective. We've had a great time looking for Christmas material that is, we hope, completely new to you. There are a few of the old favourites, of course, but some of them should surprise too: *Silent Night* in gospel style, *It came upon the midnight Clear* with the American tune or a rap song (*Rapping Paper*) about Christmas presents that is guaranteed to bring the house down! Ten of the carols have been specially composed for this book; we also give the collection a truly international flavour by including carols from fifteen countries – including Sweden, China, Puerto Rico and India – without neglecting both medieval and modern settings from all parts of the British Isles.

All the carols are written for soprano and alto, but also have an optional third part of limited range for baritone and/or low alto. The collection builds on the format of the Faber Young Voices series, but we hope that the arrangements will be used by all choirs – upper voice choirs, school choirs and adult choirs with a limited number of male singers – looking for fresh and contemporary alternatives to enliven their Christmas carol service or concert.

We hope that you have as much fun exploring this repertoire as we have had in compiling it, and that *The Faber Carol Book* becomes an essential and reliable resource for many years to come!

Gwyn Arch and Ben Parry

Gwyn Arch is one of the best-known composers and arrangers writing for young voice choirs. He has arranged many of the publications within the successful Faber Young Voices series and Choral Programme Series, and is in high demand as a conductor, adjudicator and workshop leader.

Ben Parry was a singer and arranger with the Swingle Singers and is a choral conductor based in Edinburgh, as well as one of the key teachers on the renowned Eton Choral Courses. Not only a highly popular, dynamic workshop leader and vocal coach, Ben has also contributed many arrangements to Faber Music's Choral Programme Series.

PERFORMANCE NOTES

Many of the songs and carols in this collection lend themselves naturally to the addition of instruments or percussion. We provide several optional instrument parts in the scores, but you might like to explore some of your own ideas: for example, in *O Mary, where is your baby?* you could devise a simple hand-clapping part. In *Moon Dance*, the piano/synthesiser part (the drone) is intended to imitate the sitar (an Asian lute); however, you could substitute a guitar for C and high F, with a cello playing the low F minim to great effect. If you are using the piano, experiment with the sustaining pedal, holding it down for three bars at a time. In *Shiao bao bao* the piano left-hand drone could be played instead by cello(s) and viola if the simple xylophone part is used.

Several of the items have taken traditional songs from countries across the world but have amalgamated translations of the original texts with new words celebrating the theme of Christmas. For example, the original words of the Botswana song, *Tsaba, tsaba!* advise children to take their education seriously otherwise they would run into difficulties in life. In this Christmas adaptation, the lyrics have been turned on their heads, so that it is the children this time addressing the adults and advising them to preserve the true meaning of Christmas. In performing these songs, imagine the context and the style in which they would be sung in their own countries.

Small notes throughout have been used to indicate optional alternatives for the singers. In the Baritone and/or low alto part, the small notes provide alternatives for altos unable to reach to lower notes of the baritone part.

CONTENTS

1. Starwise

Words: Patrick Rooke

Music: Gwyn Arch

Excited and fast (♩ = c.192)

ALL *mf*

SOPRANO
ALTO

BARITONE/ALTO
(optional)

mf

Excited and fast (♩ = c.192)

PIANO

mf

1. Won-der-ful news of a
2. Sud-den-ly high in the
3. Ev-'ry-one came to that

hea-ven-ly babe bring-ing peace to all peo-ple on earth.
sky a-bove shone a star bright-er than a-ny star seen.
glo-ri-fied sta-ble and lov-ing-ly of-fered a prayer.

poco rit.

S.   A.   ALL

Shep-herds had word of it;   Mon-archs soon heard of it,   heard of His
'Is-n't it fine?' they said.   'Must be a sign!' they said.   'What does it
Shep-herds were proud of Him.   Prin-ces who bowed to Him   wor-shipped Him

poco rit.

© Copyright 2001 by Faber Music Ltd.

This music is copyright. Photocopying is ILLEGAL.

*flute/violin/treble recorder, etc. *ad lib.*

shep-herds sang. Let their words ring: 'Hail to the babe.
wise men brought. Won - der - ful things, spi - ces and gold.
long a - go. Let the song ring. 'Hail to the babe.'

shep-herds sang. 'Ti - ny in - - fant
wise men brought. Won - der - ful things
long a - go. Let the song ring.

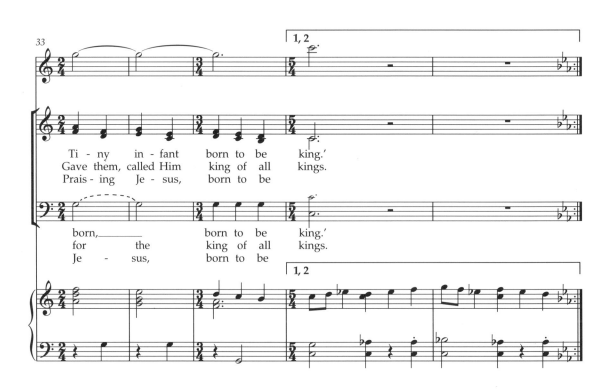

Ti - ny in - fant born to be king.'
Gave them, called Him king of all kings.
Prais - ing Je - sus, born to be

born, born to be king.'
for the king of all kings.
Je - sus, born to be

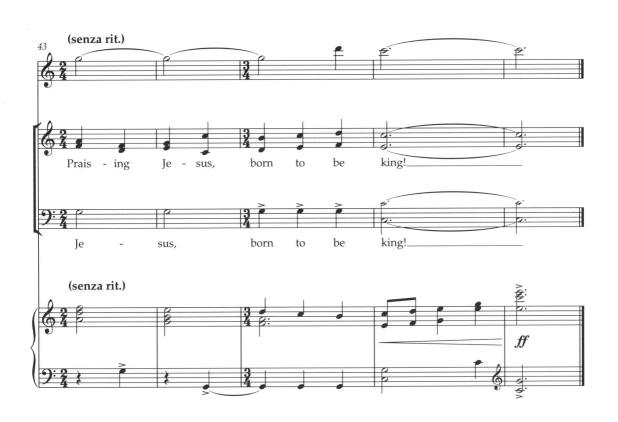

2. Sun Carol

Words tr. Ben Parry

Georgian traditional (lullaby)
arr. Ben Parry

© Copyright 2001 by Faber Music Ltd.

This music is copyright. Photocopying is ILLEGAL.

3. Fum, fum, fum

Words: Patrick Rooke and Gwyn Arch

Spanish traditional
arr. Gwyn Arch

* Sing only if there are no baritones.

© Copyright 2001 by Faber Music Ltd.

This music is copyright. Photocopying is ILLEGAL.

23

fum. Son of Ma - ry, ho - ly trea - sure, blessed are we be - yond all

fum. Son of Ma - ry, ho - ly trea - sure, blessed be - yond all

fum. Son of Ma - - - ry, Ma -

27

mea - sure. *Fum,* *fum,* *fum.*

mea - sure. *Fum* *fum,* *fum* *fum.*

-ry. *Fum* *fum,* *fum* *fum.*

4. Tàladh Chriosta

Christ's Lullaby

Words: tr. Ben Parry

Gaelic traditional (lullaby)
arr. Ben Parry

Slowly and gently (♩. = c.48)

VOICE

SOLO *(optional)* **p** *espress.*

My dar - ling, sweet and

PIANO

p *legato*

Ped._____ ∧_____ ∧*sim.*

6

trea - sure, you, my new - found joy and plea - sure, you, My gor - geous, dar-ling babe-son, you, to

11 (SOLO)

S. ALL **mp**

you I give my love. Al - le - lu - i - a, al - le - lu - i - a,

A. **mp**

Al - le - lu - i - a, al - le - lu - i - a,

B./A. (opt.) **mp**

Al - le - lu - i - a, al - le - lu - i - a,

Ped._____ ∧_____ ∧*sim.*

© Copyright 2001 by Faber Music Ltd.

This music is copyright. Photocopying is ILLEGAL.

al - le - lu - i - a, al - le - lu - i - a.

al - le - lu - i - a, al - le - lu - i - a.

al - le - lu - i - a, al - le - lu - i - a.

My gen - tle one I see you here, my heart so full of love my dear, My

ti - ny, help - less babe - son, you, so full of good, be - yond com - pare.

5. Diamond Bright

Words and music: Lin Marsh

© Copyright 2001 by Faber Music Ltd.

This music is copyright. Photocopying is ILLEGAL.

6. Angelus ad Virginem

The Angel to the Virgin

Words: Patrick Rooke

14th-century
arr. Gwyn Arch

© Copyright 2001 by Faber Music Ltd.

This music is copyright. Photocopying is ILLEGAL.

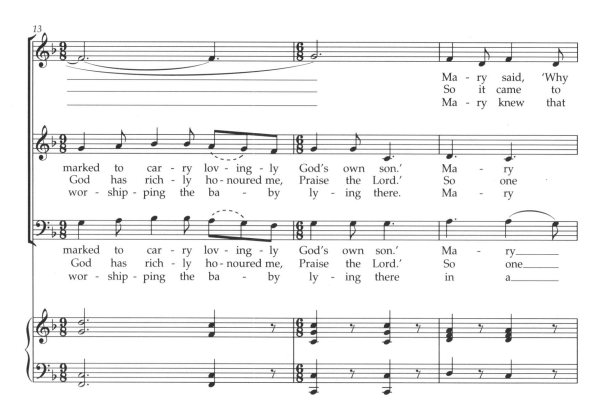

INSTRUMENTAL INTERLUDE *(optional)*

CODA

7. It came upon a midnight clear

Words: Edmund H. Sears (1810–76)

American carol, music: Richard S. Willis (1819–1900)
arr. Ben Parry

© Copyright 2001 by Faber Music Ltd.

This music is copyright. Photocopying is ILLEGAL.

on the earth,___ good - will to men From heav'n's all
man, at war___ with man, hears not The love___ song
peace shall o - ver all the earth Its an - cient

gra - cious King':___ The world in so - lemn
which___ they bring:___ O hush your noise,___ you
splen - dours fling,___ And the whole world___ give

still - ness lay To hear the an - gels sing.___
men of strife, And hear the an - gels sing!
back the song Which now the an - gels

1, 2

mf

(1, 2) *mp* (v.3 *f*) **3**

2. Still sing.___
3. For

8. Moon Dance

Words: Sue Alexander

Indian traditional (Gujarat)
arr. Gwyn Arch

* Treble recorder/Flute/Violin/Piano/Synthesiser.

† See Performance notes, p.iv.

© Copyright 2001 by Faber Music Ltd.

This music is copyright. Photocopying is ILLEGAL.

tap sticks above the head

dance be-neath the ris - ing moon that brings the hap-py news.
ce - le-brate our plea-sure in a moon-lit dance of mirth. Come and join us in the cir-cle as the

si - tar leads us in the mu-sic of the dance. Come and join us in the cir-cle as the

si - tar leads us in the mu-sic of the dance.

MELODY INSTRUMENT

Indian Bells

3. Look how the moon smiles

34

* The melody instruments may join in at any point.

9. O Mary, where is your baby?

American traditional (spiritual)
arr. Gwyn Arch

© Copyright 2001 by Faber Music Ltd.

This music is copyright. Photocopying is ILLEGAL.

36

* Sing only if there are no baritones.

10. Christmas is here again

Words: tr. Hedvig Eriksson

Swedish traditional (dance carol)
arr. Ben Parry

© Copyright 2001 by Faber Music Ltd.

This music is copyright. Photocopying is ILLEGAL.

* bb.27–31: optional altos sing canon an octave higher.

11. Silent Night

Franz Xaver Gruber (1787–1863)
arr. Gwyn Arch

© Copyright 2001 by Faber Music Ltd.

This music is copyright. Photocopying is ILLEGAL.

Christ the sa-viour is born!

Christ the sa-viour is born!

D.S. 𝄋 al ⊕ poi al Coda

CODA

(ALL)

birth.

birth.

rit.

12. Let me shine

Words and music: Mike Brewer

© Copyright 2001 Faber Music Ltd.

This music is copyright. Photocopying is ILLEGAL.

13. The Wexford Carol

Words: Dr Grattan Flood

Irish traditional
arr. Ben Parry

© Copyright 2001 by Faber Music Ltd.

This music is copyright. Photocopying is ILLEGAL.

14. When Christ was born

Words: 15th-century

Music: Ben Parry

© Copyright 2001 by Faber Music Ltd.

This music is copyright. Photocopying is ILLEGAL.

* descant optional.

15. What month was Jesus born in?

© Copyright 2001 by Faber Music Ltd.

This music is copyright. Photocopying is ILLEGAL.

16. Il est né, le divin enfant

He is born, the holy child

Words: tr. Ben Parry

French traditional
arr. Ben Parry

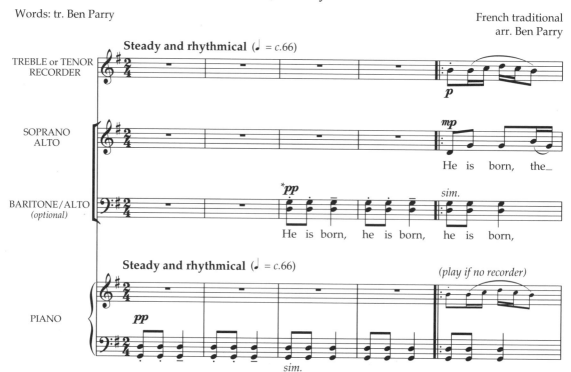

* Sing both notes if enough voices available, otherwise sing the upper note.

© Copyright 2001 by Faber Music Ltd.

This music is copyright. Photocopying is ILLEGAL.

17. A Polish Lullaby

Words: Sue Alexander

Polish traditional
arr. Gwyn Arch

© Copyright 2001 by Faber Music Ltd.

This music is copyright. Photocopying is ILLEGAL.

18. While shepherds watched their flocks

Thomas Clark (1775–1839)
arr. Gwyn Arch

© Copyright 2001 by Faber Music Ltd.

This music is copyright. Photocopying is ILLEGAL.

* In the absence of the optional part, some altos might like to sing bb. 14–17.

CODA

19.   The Warmth of Christmas

Words: Roger Kendal

Puerto Rican traditional
arr. Gwyn Arch

© Copyright 2001 by Faber Music Ltd.

This music is copyright. Photocopying is ILLEGAL.

20.   The Coventry Carol

16th-century English carol
arr. Ben Parry

© Copyright 2001 by Faber Music Ltd.

This music is copyright. Photocopying is ILLEGAL.

84

21. So many stars

Words and music: Lin Marsh

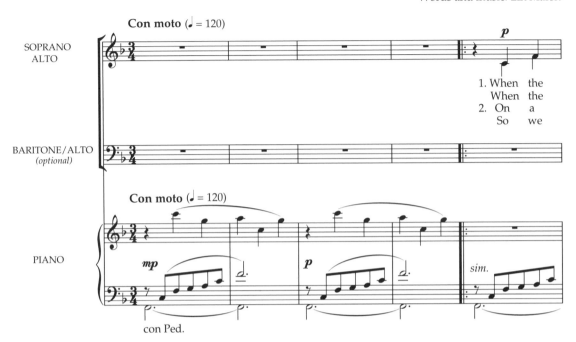

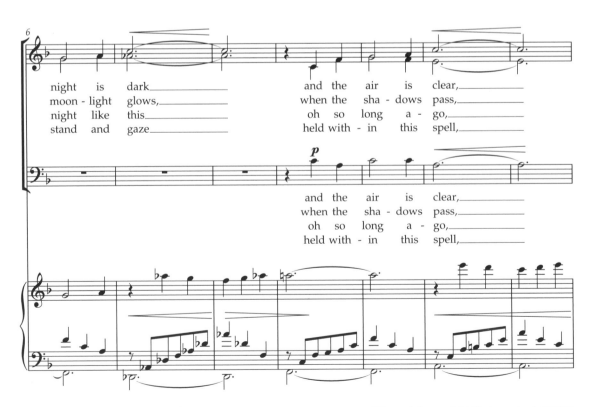

© Copyright 2001 by Faber Music Ltd.

This music is copyright. Photocopying is ILLEGAL.

Do you look up to the stars in the hea-vens, stop for a mo-ment and
Do you feel some-thing is stir-ring with-in you, stop for a mo-ment to
One spe-cial star led the way to a sta-ble, stopped for a mo-ment, its
Lost in the beau-ty of God's own cre-a-tion, hop-ing one day we'll dis-

Do you look up to the stars in the hea-vens, stop for a mo-ment and
Do you feel some-thing is stir-ring with-in you, stop for a mo-ment to
One spe-cial star led the way to a sta-ble, stopped for a mo-ment, its
Lost in the beau-ty of God's own cre-a-tion, hop-ing one day we'll dis-

won-der just why you are here?
lis-ten in-stead to your heart?
won-der-ful bless-ing to show.
-co-ver it all: who can tell?

won-der just why you are here?
lis-ten in-stead to your heart?
won-der-ful bless-ing to show.
-co-ver it all: who can tell?

for the people of Trinity United Reformed Church, Wimbledon

22. A Christmas Prayer

Words: Ceri Lewis

Music: Peter Gritton

© Copyright 2001 by Faber Music Ltd.

This music is copyright. Photocopying is ILLEGAL.

23. Baloo, Lammy

17th-century Scottish traditional
arr. Gwyn Arch

© Copyright 2001 by Faber Music Ltd.

This music is copyright. Photocopying is ILLEGAL.

24. Sister Mary had but one child

American traditional (spiritual)
arr. Gwyn Arch

Sis-ter Ma-ry had a but one child, born in Beth - le-hem, and e-ve-ry time the ba-by cried, she rocked him in a wea-ry land,

*oo_____ (oo)

* Breathe anywhere, somewhere in the *middle* of a bar.

© Copyright 2001 by Faber Music Ltd.

This music is copyright. Photocopying is ILLEGAL.

25. Ring, lovely bells

Words: tr. Hedvig Eriksson

Swedish traditional
arr. Ben Parry

© Copyright 2001 by Faber Music Ltd.

This music is copyright. Photocopying is ILLEGAL.

All the fo-rest smiles at us, and we smile back, do not o-ver-turn us on__ our__ jour-ney!
Soon we will be rest - ing by the fire-side glow, when we're there then no-one could be__ hap-pier!

fo - rest smiles and we smile back, do not o-ver-turn us on our jour-ney!
soon__ to rest by the fire - side, when we're there then no-one could be hap-pier!

Can I see a__ light that__ shines__ from a - far? Is it home or just the__
All the nor - thern lights are__ fli - ck'ring in the sky, all the me - m'ries shine so__

fire__ from a star?
dim be-fore my eyes:

26. Tsaba, tsaba!*

Watch out, watch out!

Words: Peter Gritton

Botswana traditional
arr. Peter Gritton

* See Performance notes, p.iv.

© Copyright 2001 by Faber Music Ltd.

This music is copyright. Photocopying is ILLEGAL.

* *Tsaba, amahy brakes!* = Watch out: put on the brakes! (i.e. 'stop!')

27. O, can you not hear?

Words: Ben Parry

English traditional (*Waly waly*)
arr. Ben Parry

© Copyright 2001 by Faber Music Ltd.

This music is copyright. Photocopying is ILLEGAL.

for Jahneen, Anthony and Tahir Wallen

28. Designer Christmas

Words and music: Errollyn Wallen

© Copyright 2001 by Faber Music Ltd.

This music is copyright. Photocopying is ILLEGAL.

29. Away in a manger

American carol, music: James R. Murray (1841/2–1905)
arr. Gwyn Arch

* Sing both notes if enough voices available; otherwise sing either one of the two parts.

© Copyright 2001 by Faber Music Ltd.

This music is copyright. Photocopying is ILLEGAL.

stars in the sky____ looked down where He lay, The lit - tle Lord Je - sus a -
love Thee, Lord Je - sus, look down from the sky, And stay by my cra - dle till
all the dear child - ren in Thy ten - der care, And fit us for Hea - ven to

stars in the sky____ looked down where He lay, The lit - tle Lord Je - sus a -
love Thee, Lord Je - sus, look down from the sky, And stay by my cra - dle till
all the dear child - ren in Thy ten - der care, And fit us for Hea - ven to

mm_____ mm_____

-sleep on the hay.
morn-ing is nigh.
live with Thee there.

2. The
3. Be

-sleep on the hay.
morn-ing is nigh.
live with Thee there.

2. The
3. Be

1, 2   **3**

30. Rise up shepherd and foller

American traditional (spiritual)
arr. Ben Parry

© Copyright 2001 by Faber Music Ltd.

This music is copyright. Photocopying is ILLEGAL.

31. Shiao bao bao

Little Precious

Words: Patrick Rooke

Chinese traditional (cradle song)
arr. Gwyn Arch

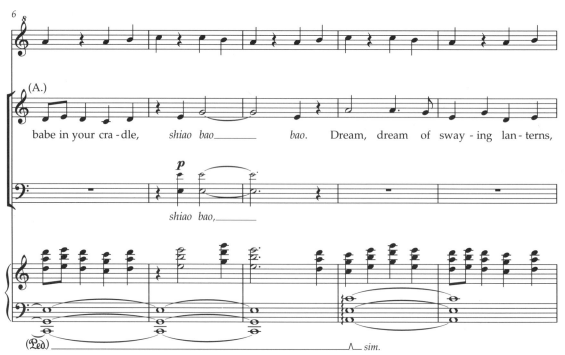

* See Performance notes, p.iv.

© Copyright 2001 by Faber Music Ltd.

This music is copyright. Photocopying is ILLEGAL.

32. Just a tale

A song for Christmas

Words: Stephen Clark

Music: Howard Goodall

Easy and flowing (♩ = c.76)

SOPRANO — *p* — It is a

ALTO — *p* — It is a

BARITONE/ALTO (optional) — *p* — It is a

PIANO — *p* — con Ped.

sto - ry, a sim - ple sto - ry,____ a sto - ry told in lands we've ne - ver
ba - by, a new-born ba - by,____ a ba - by bathed in swathes of love and

sto - ry, a sim - ple sto - ry,____ a sto - ry told in lands we've ne - ver
ba - by, a new-born ba - by,____ a ba - by bathed in swathes of love and

sto - ry, a sim - ple sto - ry____ told in lands we've ne - ver
ba - by, a new-born ba - by____ bathed in swathes of love and

© Copyright 2001 by Faber Music Ltd.

This music is copyright. Photocopying is ILLEGAL.

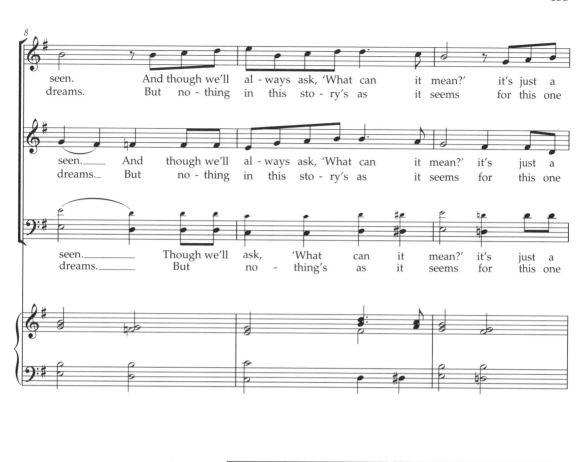

* Sing melody if there are no baritones.

134

33. Child of God

American traditional (spiritual)
arr. Ben Parry

* Or hum (*mm*).

© Copyright 2001 by Faber Music Ltd.

This music is copyright. Photocopying is ILLEGAL.

* Or hum (*mm*).

34. Cysga di, fy mhlentyn tlws

Sleep away, my gentle child

Words: Sue Alexander

Welsh traditional
arr. Gwyn Arch

* Optional instrumental interlude. Oboe/Flute/Violin/Recorder, *etc.* If this isn't used, use 𝄋 repeat.

© Copyright 2001 by Faber Music Ltd.

This music is copyright. Photocopying is ILLEGAL.

35. La Jornada

The Journey

Words: Ben Parry

Spanish traditional
arr. Ben Parry

© Copyright 2001 by Faber Music Ltd.

This music is copyright. Photocopying is ILLEGAL.

CODA

36. Now and then Christmas

Words: Richard Williams

Music: Gwyn Arch

*All solos could be sung by small groups.

© Copyright 2001 by Faber Music Ltd.

This music is copyright. Photocopying is ILLEGAL.

37. The Linden Tree Carol

Words: tr. Ben Parry

German traditional
arr. Ben Parry

Flowing (♩. = c.44)

SOPRANO

oo

ALTO

oo

BARITONE/ALTO
(optional)

oo

Flowing (♩. = c.44)

PIANO

mp espressivo

con Ped.

S.

SOLO (optional)
mp espress.

1. In heav'n there stood a Lin - den Tree, and though its boughs were
4. 'So be God's will' then Ma - ry cried, 'ac - cord - ing to your

2nd time to Coda

la - den, the an - gels sang, 'No flower shall be like that of one fair
sto - ry.' And Ga - bri - el then left her side, to spread this news of

2nd time to Coda

© Copyright 2001 by Faber Music Ltd.

This music is copyright. Photocopying is ILLEGAL.

38. A merry Christmas

English traditional
arr. Gwyn Arch

© Copyright 2001 by Faber Music Ltd.

This music is copyright. Photocopying is ILLEGAL.

all like lots of fig-gy pud-ding so bring, bring,— bring it out here. Good ti-dings we bring to you and your kin, we wish you a ve-ry mer-ry Christ-mas and a hap-py— New Year. And we won't go 'til we

39. Rapping Paper

Words and music: Ben Parry

* The text should be recited loudly and with great energy. Let your hair down!

© Copyright 2001 by Faber Music Ltd.   This music is copyright. Photocopying is ILLEGAL.

40. Gaudete!

Rejoice!

Words: 14th-century
tr. John Parry

16th-century, *Piae Cantiones*
arr. Ben Parry

* Pause last time only, with drum roll.
†A prophet of the Old Testament, pronounced *E-zee-kee-el*!

© Copyright 2001 by Faber Music Ltd.

This music is copyright. Photocopying is ILLEGAL.

ORIGINAL PIECES

MEDIEVAL/RENAISSANCE

EUROPEAN CAROLS

AMERICAN CAROLS

BRITISH ISLES TRADITIONAL

EUROPEAN TRADITIONAL

CAUCASIAN TRADITIONAL

AMERICAN TRADITIONAL (SPIRITUALS)

INDIAN TRADITIONAL

LATIN AMERICAN TRADITIONAL

AFRICAN TRADITIONAL

CHINESE TRADITIONAL

INDEX OF FIRST LINES AND TITLES